Traveling Light

Stories & Drawings
For a Quiet Mind

StoryPeople
Decorah

ISBN 0-9642660-9-1

The people in this book, if at one time real, are now entirely fictitious, having been subjected to a combination of a selective memory and a fertile imagination. Any resemblance to real people you might know, even if they are the author's relatives, is entirely coincidental, and is a reminder that you are imagining the incidents in this book as much as the author. (By the way, the "she" is not who you think it is, either. So, give it up...)

StoryPeople
P.O. Box 7
Decorah, IA 52101
USA
563.382.8060
563.382.0263 FAX
800.476.7178

storypeople@storypeople.com
www.storypeople.com

First Edition: *May, 2003*

Produced by West Coast Print Center, Oakland, California
on 30% tree-free kenaf / 70% recycled, chlorine-free archival text paper

To my sons, for their love & curiosity & outrageously comic view of the future we're all making together & to Ellen, for the way she holds love & home & a world that works for everyone in a heart as strong & beautiful as life itself

Other books by Brian Andreas available
from StoryPeople Press:

Mostly True
Still Mostly True
Going Somewhere Soon
Strange Dreams
Hearing Voices
Story People
Trusting Soul

Traveling Light

Introduction

I like to travel. Or maybe that's not exactly right. Maybe it's more like this: as I go on, my idea of home is expanding & I can't wait to find out how big it will be. There's a side of home that means sitting on the kitchen counter, between the children & dishes & conversation & the smell of Earl Grey tea. There's another, completely different side that is all the places I've been. The places I've lived. The places I've visited. Even the places I've yet to find.

They're all home. I carry them with me everywhere I go & there's no telling when a memory of my boyhood in Chicago will cross paths with my adult life as I ferry one of the kids to some place or another. Or the smells of some new dish my younger son is throwing together on the stove suddenly reminding me of that lively Cuban restaurant Ellen & I found on a walk through Atlanta fifteen years ago.

I like to collect memories of people & things. For all my love of travel, I have no interest in collecting stuff from foreign lands. I'm not someone who brings back a container load of bright colored blankets, or realistic carvings of little Buddhas on pieces of driftwood, or even loaves of authentic sourdough bread. The most I usually bring back is chocolate & stories. I like to travel light.

It's enough for me to have memories of someone, or somewhere I love. The way sometimes when you catch it just right, our spice cabinet smells like my great-aunt's kitchen on a Sunday morning. The way my elder son puts his hands on his hips just like Ellen when he's surveying the scene right before he jumps in. The way you can just barely see where the boys wrote their names on the side of the big pine table. Memories make the world home.

The truth is, I like to be in the middle of my day & stop to remember the way the morning fog in Santa Barbara scatters suddenly, like a flock of startled birds & there is only you & the ocean, as blue as any ocean can be. At odd times, I think of the small Chinese woman on a side street in Hong Kong, taking down a freshly slaughtered goose with one hand & chattering into a cellphone held in the other. Now & then, I watch a hot wind curling dust into little funnels & I'm back in Mexico, on a steep cobblestone street that curves like a dry riverbed through a canyon of yellow houses. I notice the light glint on the river outside our house & in a moment, I'm there on a stone bridge in Paris, letting flower petals drop like wishes into the Seine.

It's no coincidence that this book is called 'Traveling Light'. Memories weigh nothing & yet, they feel like they're everything. They surround us & wash through us & tag along as we go through our lives. They're filled with laughter & exuberant gestures & at the same time, they are as quiet as the night wind. I've folded many of them neatly into stories here, so we can be ready at a moment's notice to travel when a new adventure calls.

Come & join me. Let's see what kind of home this wide world offers. It'll be great fun. I've already packed the book with most everything we'll need...

With love,

Brian Andreas
On David's birthday
28 March 2003

In those days,
we finally chose
to walk like giants
& hold the world
in arms grown strong
with love

& there may be
many things we forget
in the days to come,

but this
will not be
one of them.

Awakening

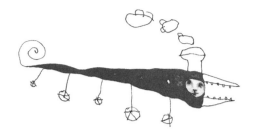

carries a lot of suitcases
but all of them are empty
because she's expecting
to completely fill them
with life by the end of
this trip

& then she'll come home
& sort everything out
& do it all again

Veteran Traveller

I'd like to think
that things are
getting better,
he said, but
my eyes are
getting worse,
so maybe I miss
a lot.

Blind Spot

My life had
such potential,
she told me,
before I found out
how much work
was involved.

Potential Energy

I can imagine it
working out
perfectly, I said.

    I can't, she said

& I said no wonder
you're so stressed

Stress Management

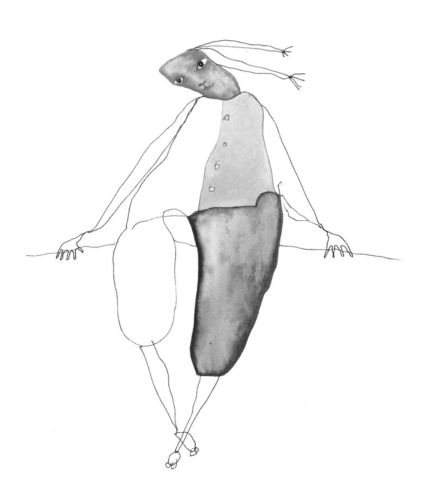

It's a very fragile
world, she told us,
so walk carefully
everywhere you go

& we promised
to remember
for as long
as we could.

Fragile World

sending postcards
to himself saying
'Wish you were here'

so when he gets
back home
he doesn't
forget

Being There

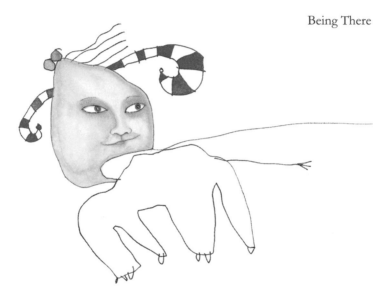

I just tell them
to do things they
already want
to do, she said,
& even then,
it's like pulling
teeth.

Opposition

We're already
in the New Age,
she said.

What does that
mean? I said.

It means we can
stop waiting &
start living,
she said.

But after she left,
I still waited
a little more
just to be
safe.

New Age

It was a day filled with the glow
of ordinary things
& we passed them quietly
from hand to hand
for a long time

& someone said he had picked
a perfect day to be born

& I think all of us
felt the same

Perfect Day

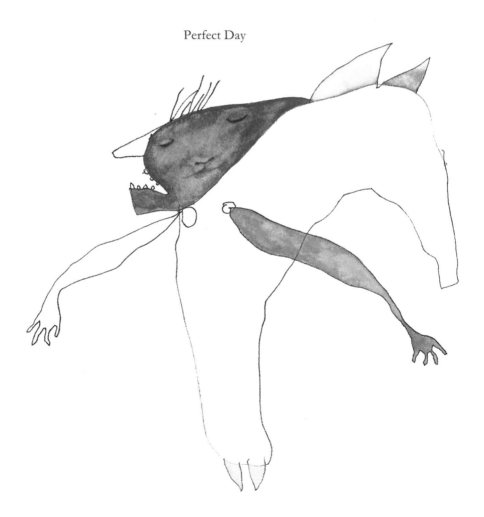

Anyone can slay a dragon,
he told me, but try waking up
every morning & loving
the world all over again.

That's what takes a real hero

Real Hero

I've had some of
my best conversations
with strangers,
she said, because
they have no idea
who they're
dealing with.

No Idea

not very good
with love poems
to the world,
so they usually
just end up saying,
How's it going?
to everyone
they meet

Love Poems

This is a creature
on fire with love,
but it's still scary
since most people
think love only looks
like one thing,

instead of
the whole world

Creature on Fire

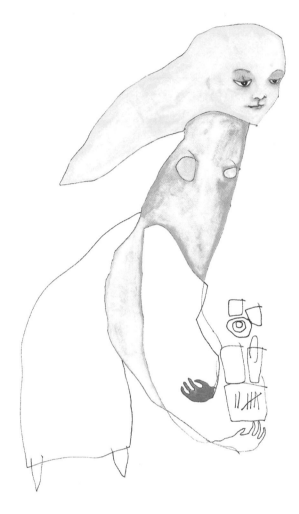

This is a giant block
of whatever is most difficult
for you to carry & trust me on this,
you'll carry it more times
than you can count
until you decide that's exactly
what you want to do most

& then it won't weigh
a thing anymore.

Weight Training

I'm waiting for sloth
to come back in style,
he said.

You may wait a long
time, I said.

That's **OK**, he said,
I can use the practice.

Sloth

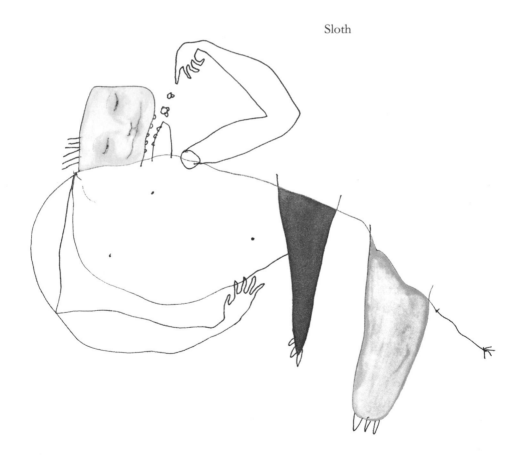

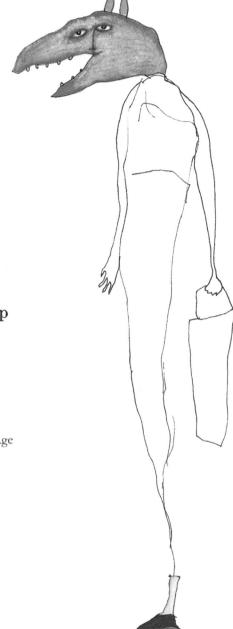

Is willing to accept
that she creates
her own reality
except for some
of the parts
where she can't help
but wonder
what the hell
she was thinking

Almost New Age

THINGS TO KNOW
ABOUT THE FUTURE

It doesn't have to
look any particular
way, but around here,
if it doesn't, a lot of
people will never
speak to you again.

Known Future

for a long time,
there were only your
footprints & laughter
in our dreams,

& even from
such small things,
we knew we couldn't wait
to love you forever

Such Small Things

I don't know how long
I can do this, he said.
I think the universe
has different plans
for me

& we sat there in silence

 & I thought to myself
that this is the thing
we all come to
& this is the thing
we all fight
& if we are lucky
enough to lose,
our lives
become beautiful
with mystery
again

& I sat there silent
because that is not
something
that can be said.

Different Plans

I have so much
less stress,
he said, now that
I've given up
on ambition

Stress Reduction

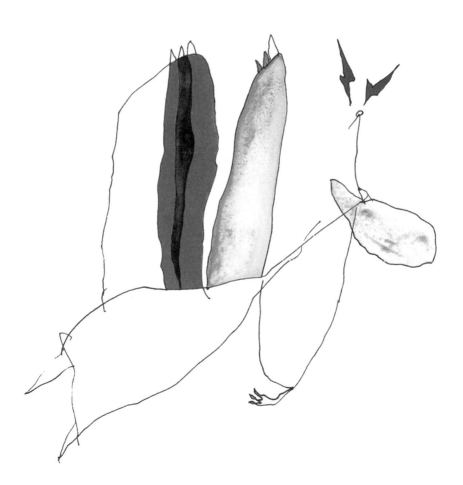

This is just one
of those lives you try
& get through, she said.

I'm hoping for better luck
next time.

Better Luck

I think if I was a woman,
he told me, I'd have sex
a lot more than most
women I know

& I'd definitely
stay away from people
like me **&** my friends.

Discretion

What are the rules? I said

& she said, Do exactly what I want
whenever I want, make no demands
of me whatsoever, & love me forever,
no questions asked.

& I said, How do I win?

& she said, You don't understand.
I'm the only one who wins

& then she laughed &
clapped her hands.

Isn't it a great game?
she said.

Great Game

Of course, I want to
save the world, she said,
but I was hoping to do it
from the comfort
of my regular life.

Regular Life

I read somewhere
that if given a choice
between sex
& peace of mind,
she said, most people
would choose peace.

Personally, I said,
I do fine with
a little anxiety.

Clear Choice

I'm a Catholic, she said,
so I know about suffering.

I'm a homeowner, I said.

She nodded. So, you
understand, she said.

Like-Minded Souls

he looks fierce
mainly because
he hates the beginning
of winter & the only
thing that seems
to help is gritting
your teeth

Winter Cure

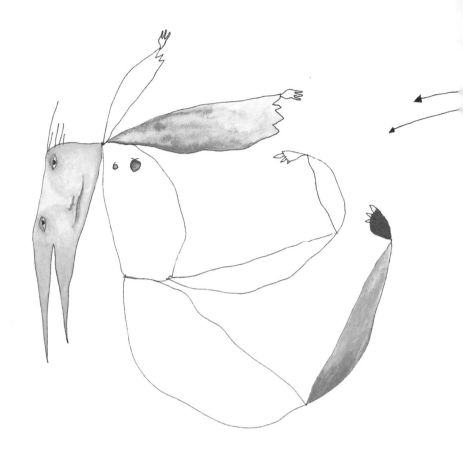

What are you
good at? I said

& she said,
Mainly life.
I work best with
 stuff that has
a high tolerance
for mistakes.

High Tolerance

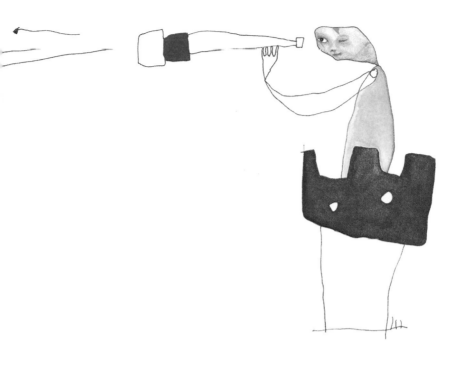

What if we all got along
& people loved each other
& sang songs about peace?
he said. Would that be
a good world?

& I said I didn't know about that,
but it would be a good summer camp

& he looked at me & shook his head
& said, It's no wonder you're
leaving us with such a mess.

Happy Camper

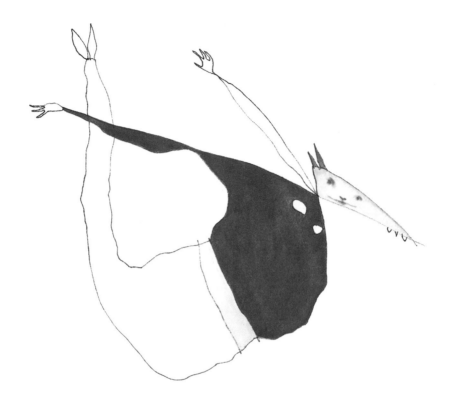

impossible yoga position
but she likes to have goals
that no one else can imagine,
so they'll shut up about
how they understand
exactly what she's
going through

Impossible Position

I understand
it's a long road
to peace, he said,
but I'm still hoping
to get a ride
part way
because I'm so
out of shape
from the 90's.

Long Road

What would it take
for world peace? I said.

Is there a right answer? he said.

No, I said.

Oh good, he said. I thought this
was going to be one of your
love-your-little-brother talks.

Right Answer

resorting to
connecting the dots
this morning because
it was a long night
& he's needing
to do something
really simple
to get started
again

Connect the Dots

I'm an animal lover
in the abstract, he said.

What does that mean? I said.

It means I try not to think
about them a whole lot,
because pet hair makes me
queasy.

Abstract Love

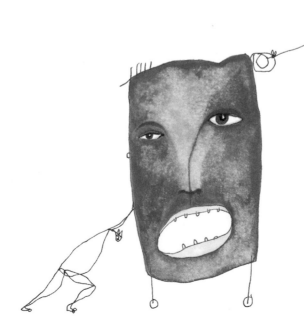

except for the running
naked through the forest,
there's not a lot I miss

Old Ways

Destiny?
There's only your time
& then there's
not-your-time,
he said.

All the rest is made up
to keep you busy.

Destiny

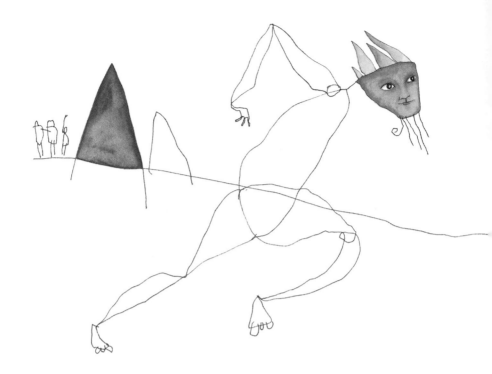

No hurt survives
for long without
our help, she said

& then she kissed
me & sent me out
to play again
for the rest
of my life.

Out to Play

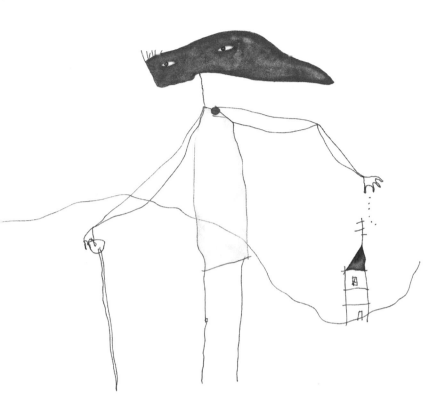

We listened as he played
the guitar & sang old love songs

& then there was a moment
we looked at each other

& discovered we were
much younger than other
people might suspect

& it was good to know
we had that much more time
together

Old Love Songs

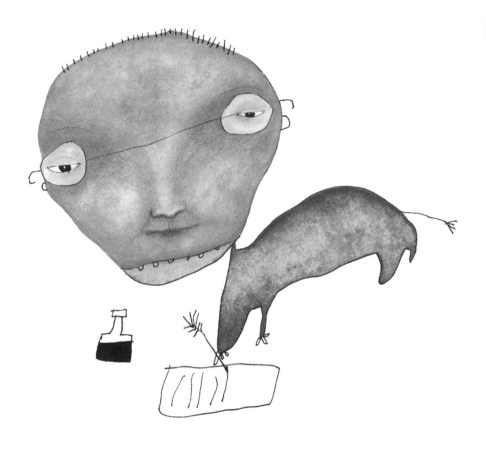

Often, I write all day long
with white ink on white paper,
late into the night,
until it is all I can do
to feel the letters
curving to earth
from the tip of the pen

& then, I fall asleep.
dreaming of running,
or maybe driving
in a car the color of water

& I wake the next day
remembering nothing
& I gather the stack of paper
& a pen of black
on the desk in front of me
& the words begin
to dance over the page
like long legged insects
across a still lake
& the words in white
whisper behind & underneath
the new day

If there is any secret
to this life I live, this is it:
the sound of what cannot be seen
sings within everything that can.

& there is nothing more to it than that.

Nothing More

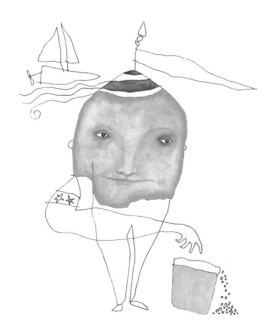

I'm at that point
in the day where
I'm tired of myself,
she said,
so if you
don't mind,
I'm going to be
someone else
until bedtime

& we had a lovely
time together,
my new friend & I

New Friend

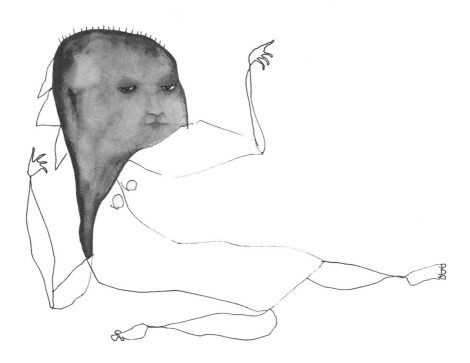

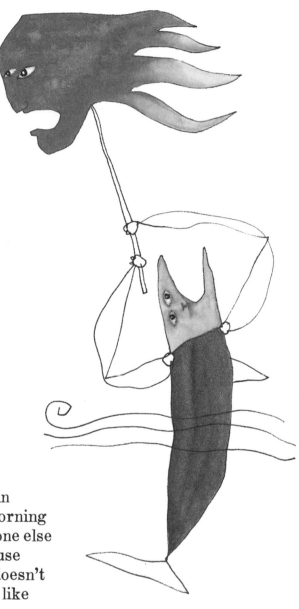

I try & get
a lot of living in
early in the morning
before everyone else
gets up, because
after that, it doesn't
seem so much like
living as it does
putting up with
stuff.

Early Life

Your job
is to focus
on my personal
happiness,
she said,

& I've got big plans,
so break time
is over.

Big Plans

If I have to choose,
my son said, I'll take
them all.

That's no choice, I said.

Obviously, he said,
you've forgotten
how choice works.

Best Choice

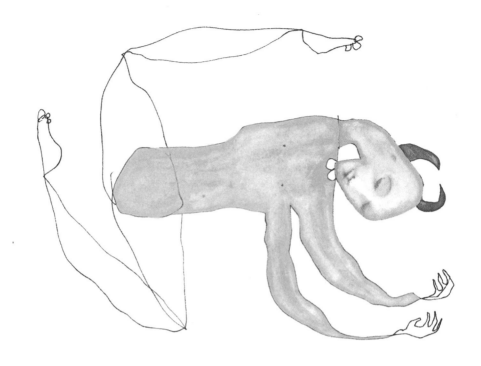

I don't believe
in love, he said

& I nodded
& said I'd heard
that argument
before & it
always ends
badly

& he couldn't
think of another
thing to say.

Bad Argument

This is a blank map
that lets you go
as far as you want
in any direction,
with no questions
asked,

but it's no help at all
if you want to know
if you're going
the right way.

Blank Map

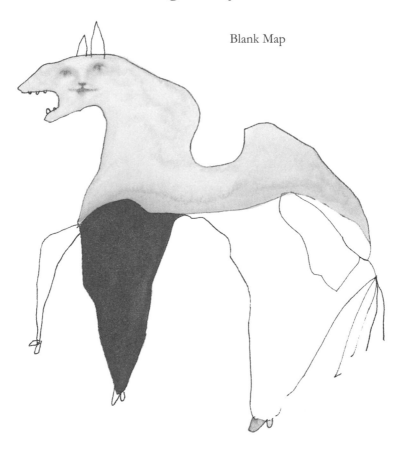

I try not
to think
too much,
he said,
so my mind
is ready
for whatever
comes up.

Preparation

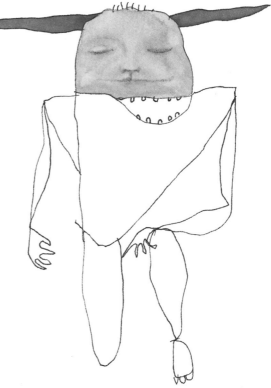

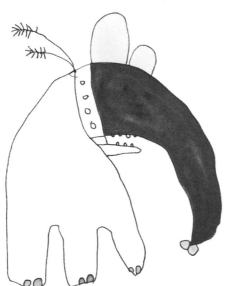

finally realizes
that all the chaos
is what makes
tea worth it

Final Reward

I bet we could
all live in peace
for a long time,
as long as everyone
stayed out of my
way, she said.

I'd hate to be
the one to ruin it.

Wide Berth

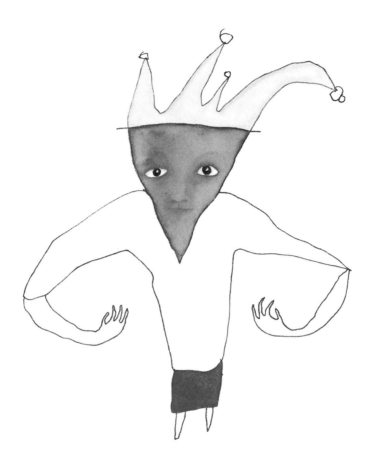

My favorite thing
is saying something
true, he said,

but I'm a lot
younger than you
& don't have
to worry so much
about my reputation.

Something True

I don't have
a whole lot
of excuses
for what's
gone wrong
with my life,
she said.

But the ones
I do have are
really good.

Really Good

not exactly
schizophrenic
in the classical sense,

but close enough
that people give him
all the room he needs
on the sidewalk

Close Enough

trying to follow
in the footsteps
of the masters,

but it's a lot harder
than it looks because
even though they had
the same size feet
as us, they weren't
looking down
the whole time
while they walked
to make sure
they were
doing it right

Strict Followers

How's it going? I said

& she said it was all going
perfectly,

unless I'd heard
differently.

Idle Chatter

Everywhere's
a small town,
she said, if you
do something
that bothers
enough people.

Small Town

It's much easier,
he told me, if
you like the parts
you like & you like
the parts you don't
like.

Is that some Eastern
thing? I said

& he said not really
since he was from Idaho
& it worked there
just fine.

Western Mysticism

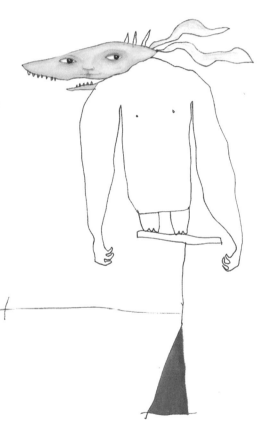

I know I promised
I wouldn't complain,
she said,

but I'm not ready
to start just yet.

Coming Soon

I like to sit
quietly in public
places, she said,
to make up for being
so obnoxious in private.

Public Face

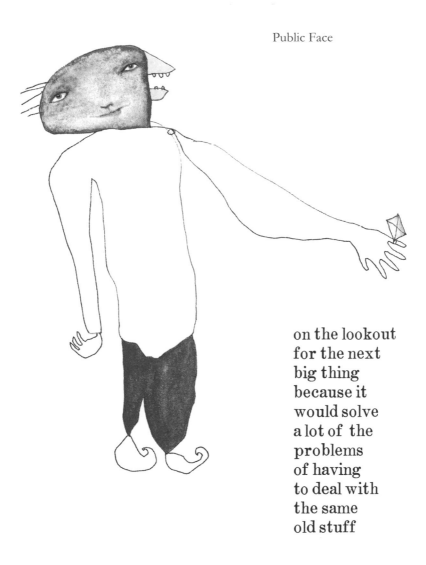

on the lookout
for the next
big thing
because it
would solve
a lot of the
problems
of having
to deal with
the same
old stuff

Next Big Thing

There are moments
when I'm completely
at peace, but it's
usually before my
children wake up

& they'll have
none of that.

Timing

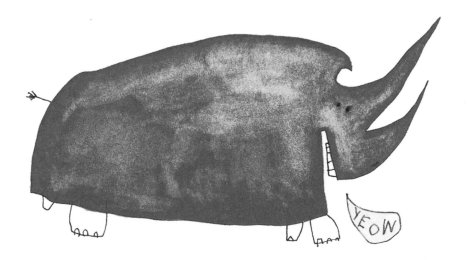

YEOW

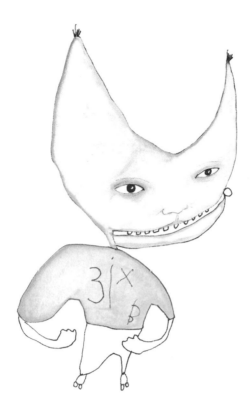

Does Santa get to do
as much PlayStation
as he wants? he said

& I said nobody gets to do
as much of anything as
they want, or the economy
would grind to a halt

& he looked at me & said,
That was a simple yes
or no question, Dad.

Too Many Words

I'm not sure
how it's going
to turn out,
except I'll die
in the end,
she said.

So, really, what
could go wrong?

Perfect Ending

I've never worried
about getting older,
he said.

I've been too busy
worrying about
getting caught.

Getting Caught

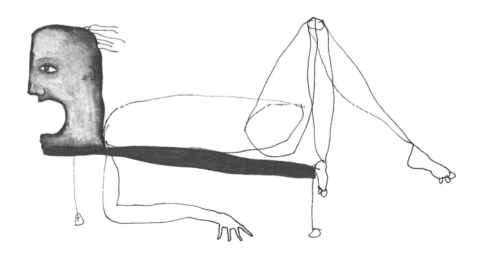

When I was young,
I used to wear
my father's shoes
& stomp around,
making the world
a better place
for us all

& today I see I'm
not the only one
who did that

& those shoes aren't
anywhere big enough
for who we are now

Bigger Shoes

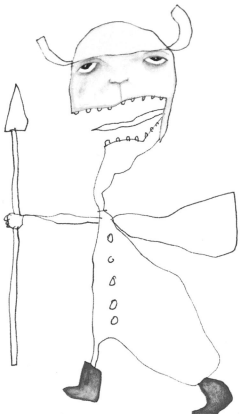

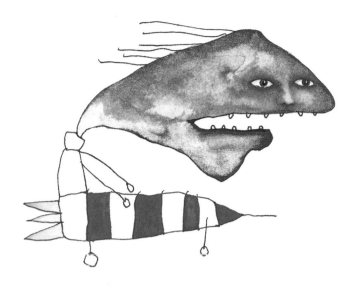

That was the day
the ancient songs
of blood & war
spilled from
a hole in the sky

& there was a long moment
as we listened & fell silent
in our grief

& then one by one,
we stood tall
& came together
& began to sing
of life & love &
all that is good & true

& I will never forget that day
when the ancient songs died
because there was no one
in the world to sing them.

Ancient Songs

I don't think of it
as working for
world peace, he said.

I think of it as
just trying to
get along in a
really big strange
family.

Big Strange Family

How many people
can you love before
it's too much? she said

& I said I didn't think
there was any
real limit as long
as you didn't care if
they loved you back

Real Limit

I'm not that good
at live & let live,
she told me, when
it's just as easy
to avoid

& then I don't even
have to think about it.

Easy Option

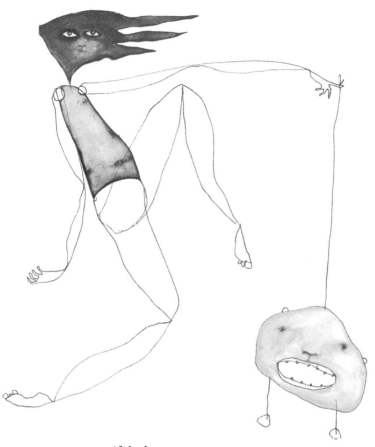

this is one
of the exact centers
of the universe

& it's in charge
of a lot of the beautiful
& amazing things
we'll take for granted
in the future

Exact Centers

What color are souls?
she said

& I said, Color isn't
that much of an issue
when you're
talking souls.

Color Blind

There was a boy
with skin as dark
as the earth

& a girl with eyes
as blue
as the deep

& they loved each other
so well that people could
not tell them apart,
for in their hearts,
there was
no difference
between them.

No Difference

I have a friend who
reads people's auras.
He sees all sorts of colors
like green & red & purple.
He says anyone can do it.
All it takes is forgetting
everything you think
you know & just looking.

I've tried it & even though
I haven't seen any
colors yet, everyone
I meet looks so beautiful
when I stop knowing
everything, that it's
pretty hard to go back
to the old way.

Beautiful People

Does everyone seem
taller than usual? she said

& I said that's what
happens when you stop
pretending you don't care.

Taller than Usual

You're not going to see
people like this again
for a long time, he said

& I said I always saw
people like this

& he looked at me for
a moment & said,
You're not from
around here,
are you?

Sightseeing

they don't have
very long memories,
so every morning
seems like a miracle

One A Day

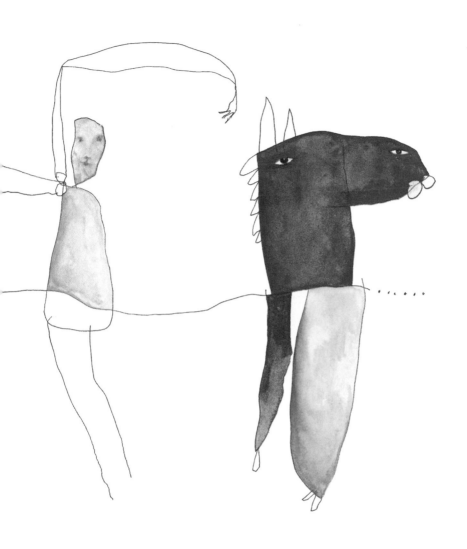

I hope it will be said
we taught them
to stand
tall & proud,
even in the face of history

& the future was made
new & whole for us all,
one child at a time.

One Child

You may not remember
the time you let me go first.

Or the time you dropped back
to tell me it wasn't that far to go.

Or the time you waited
at the crossroads for me
to catch up.

You may not remember
any of those, but I do
& this is what I have to say to you:

today, no matter what it takes,
we ride home together.

Riding Home

About the Artist

I've been remembering the future through my art & stories since 1993. I suppose that doesn't make any sense. Remembering the future is my shorthand way of saying that we all have a hand in how the future turns out. The future I imagine for you & me & all the children of the world is one that's filled with laughter & music & love, played full out. It's the only thing that makes sense to me any more.

I came to this almost by accident. I've been a playwright, waiter, tennis player, chef, contract archaeologist, accountant, systems analyst & computer programmer, among other things. For a long time, I thought I'd be a famous marble sculptor, but I always wanted to explain what was going on in my pieces. I'd attach little explanations to them, or I'd surround them with stories. With very little regard for my future plans, people ignored my sculpture & just sat around reading the words. Fortunately, I figured out that I actually liked making up stories more than carving marble.

What else? We've raised two boys. We've travelled. We've moved cross-country several times. I collected a couple of degrees in there, too. I graduated from Luther College in Decorah, Iowa with a BA in various things & I've got an MFA in Fibre & Mixed Media (in case you think I'm just one of those popular artists who can't cut it in the real world of academia) from JFK University in Orinda, California.

We live in Saint Paul, Minnesota, a stone's throw from the Arctic Circle (if you can throw about 3500 miles or so). I complain without cease about winter. It's to the point where my whole family completely ignores me when I talk about moving someplace warmer. I think this is a sign that our children are growing up with a healthy sense of self-preservation, so we must be doing something right.

This is my seventh book. People often ask which is my favorite. This is it. Hands down. May it open your heart to the world...

About StoryPeople

StoryPeople has come to mean many things. StoryPeople can be the wood sculptures created by Brian Andreas. They can be one of the hundreds of his colorful story prints. They're the community of people on the web site who share their own stories as they make sense of the world we're making together & they're any of the hundreds of thousands of people worldwide who have come to know & love his work.

StoryPeople is also the name we give to the company of friends & co-workers who make it all possible. From our small town in Iowa, we distribute Brian Andreas' stories to galleries & bookstores all over the planet. We play with the web, imagining, almost daily, new ways to bring the stories to more people. We believe in the power of stories to transform our world & we believe now is the time, more than ever before. Our business is to give our world & ourselves tools to imagine & create & heal. Stories that cherish the quiet moments. Stories of a world that works for everyone. Stories about a world worth saving.

The sculptures, the prints & the books are available in galleries, gift stores & bookstores throughout the US, Canada & the EU (along with a few others scattered about the world) & on our web site. Please feel free to call, or write, for more information, or drop in on the web at **www.storypeople.com**

StoryPeople
P.O. Box 7
Decorah, IA 52101
USA

800.476.7178
563.382.8060
563.382.0263 FAX

orders@storypeople.com